U.S. Department
of Transportation

**Federal Aviation
Administration**

FAA-S-8081-9E

T0015155

FLIGHT INSTRUCTOR INSTRUMENT
Practical Test Standards
for
Airplane Rating and Helicopter Rating

November 2023

Flight Standards Service
Washington, DC 20591

Foreword

FAA-S-8081-9E, Flight Instructor Instrument Practical Test Standards for Airplane Rating and Helicopter Rating is published by the FAA to establish the standards for flight instructor instrument practical test for airplane and helicopter ratings.

FAA-S-8081-9E supersedes FAA-S-8081-9D, Flight Instructor Instrument Practical Test Standards for Airplane and Helicopter with Changes 1 & 2, dated July 2010.

Major Enhancements

- All references were reviewed and updated throughout the PTS.
- Changed "cockpit" to "flight deck" throughout the PTS.
- The following changes were made to the Introduction:
  - Updated reference list in "PTS Description" section
  - Updated "Abbreviations/Acronyms" section
  - Updated "Practical Test Prerequisites" section
  - Updated "Aircraft and Equipment Requirements" section
  - Added "Evaluator Responsibility" section
  - Updated Task Table
  - Updated Checklists
- Single-Pilot Resource Management sub paragraph 1-6 was removed.
- Appendix 2 – Non-FSTD Device Credit was removed.
- Appendix 3 – Judgement Assessment Matrix was removed.

Table of Contents

Introduction.. 7
General Information... 7
PTS Concept 7
PTS Description 7
Abbreviations/Acronyms... 9
Use of the PTS 11
Special Emphasis Areas 12
Aircraft and Equipment Requirements 13
Use of FAA-Approved FSTD 14
Evaluator Responsibility 15
Flight Instructor Responsibility 17
Satisfactory Performance..18
Unsatisfactory Performance..19
Letter of Discontinuance...19
ADM, Risk Management, CRM, SRM 19
Applicant's Use of Checklists 20
Use of Distractions During Practical Tests 20
Positive Exchange of Flight Controls.............................. 20
Emphasis on Attitude Instrument Flying and Partial Panel Skills...21
Addition of an Instrument Rating to a Flight Instructor Certificate. 22
Renewal or Reinstatement of a Flight Instructor 23

CHECKLISTS

Applicant's Practical Test Checklist................................24
Evaluator's Practical Test Checklist............................... 25

AREAS OF OPERATION

I. FUNDAMENTALS OF INSTRUCTING

A. Learning Process... 27
B. Human Behavior and Effective Communication 27
C. Teaching Process 28
D. Teaching Methods... 28
E. Critique and Evaluation.. 28
F. Flight Instructor Characteristics and Responsibilities............... 29
G. Planning Instructional Activity 29

II. TECHNICAL SUBJECT AREAS

A. Aircraft Flight Instruments and Navigation Equipment 30
B. Aeromedical Factors 31
C. Regulations and Publications Related to IFR Operations 31
D. Logbook Entries Related to Instrument Instruction................... 32

III. PREFLIGHT PREPARATION

A. Weather Information 33
B. Cross-Country Flight Planning....................................... 33
C. Instrument Flight deck Check 34

IV. PREFLIGHT LESSON ON A MANEUVER TO BE PERFORMED IN FLIGHT

A. Maneuver Lesson 35

V. AIR TRAFFIC CONTROL CLEARANCES AND PROCEDURES

A. Air Traffic Control Clearances.................................... 36
B. Compliance With Departure, En Route, and Arrival
Procedures and Clearances................................... 36

VI. FLIGHT BY REFERENCE TO INSTRUMENTS

A. Straight-and-Level Flight 38
B. Turns 38
C. Change of Airspeed in Straight-and-Level and Turning Flight.. 39
D. Constant Airspeed Climbs and Descents 40
E. Constant Rate Climbs and Descents.. 40
F. Timed Turns to Magnetic Compass Headings 41
G. Steep Turns 42
H. Recovery From Unusual Flight Attitudes 43

VII. NAVIGATION AIDS

A. Intercepting and Tracking Navigational Systems and DME
Arcs 44
B. Holding Procedures 45

VIII. INSTRUMENT APPROACH PROCEDURES

A. Nonprecision Instrument Approach 46
B. Precision Instrument Approach 47
C. Missed Approach.. 48
D. Circling Approach (Airplane) 49
E. Landing From a Straight-In Approach....................................... 50

IX. EMERGENCY OPERATIONS

A. Loss of Communications 51
B. Approach With Loss of Primary Flight Instrument Indicators 51
C. Engine Failure During Straight-and-Level Flight and Turns
(Multiengine) 52
D. Instrument Approach—One Engine Inoperative (Multiengine). 53

X. POSTFLIGHT PROCEDURES

A. Checking Instruments and Equipment...................................... 55

APPENDIX 1: FSTD CREDIT

Task vs. Flight Simulation Training Device (FSTD) Credit............. 56
Use of Chart 56
Flight Task - FSTD Level 57

Introduction

General Information

The FAA has developed the PTS for use by FAA inspectors and evaluators when conducting the flight instructor practical test for instrument-airplane rating and instrument-helicopter rating. Instructors should use this PTS when preparing applicants for practical tests. Applicants should be familiar with this PTS and refer to these standards during their training.

Throughout this PTS the following titles will be referred to as an evaluator: ASI, pilot examiner (other than administrative pilot examiners), TCE, chief instructor, assistant chief instructor, or check instructor of pilot school holding examining authority.

Information considered directive in nature is described in this PTS in terms such as "shall" and "must," indicating the actions are mandatory. Guidance information is described in terms such as "should" and "may," indicating the actions are desirable or permissive, but not mandatory.

This PTS is available for download, in PDF format, from www.faa.gov.

Comments regarding this PTS may be emailed to acsptsinquiries@faa.gov.

PTS Concept

14 CFR part 61 specifies the subject areas in which knowledge and skill must be demonstrated by the applicant before the issuance of a certificate. The practical test standards contain the Areas of Operation and specific Tasks in which competency shall be demonstrated. The FAA will revise this PTS whenever it is determined that changes are needed in the interest of safety. Per 14 CFR part 61, section 61.43, adherence to the practical test standards is mandatory.

PTS Description

The Flight Instructor Instrument Practical Test Standards for Airplane Rating and Helicopter Rating include the AREAS OF OPERATION and TASKS required for the issuance of an initial flight instructor instrument certificate and for the addition of a category and/or class rating to that certificate.

AREAS OF OPERATION are phases of the practical test arranged in a logical sequence within each standard. They begin with Fundamentals of Instructing and end with Postflight Procedures. The evaluator, however, may conduct the practical test in any sequence that will result in a complete and efficient test; however, **the ground portion of the practical test must be completed prior to the flight portion.**

TASKS are titles of knowledge areas, flight procedures, or maneuvers appropriate to an AREA OF OPERATION.

NOTE is used to emphasize special considerations required in the AREA OF OPERATION or TASK.

The Objective lists the important elements that must be satisfactorily performed to demonstrate competency in a TASK. The Objective includes:

1. Specifically what the applicant should be able to do;
2. The conditions under which the TASK is to be performed;
3. The acceptable performance standards; and
4. Safety considerations, when applicable.

REFERENCE(S) identifies the publication(s) that describe(s) the TASK. Descriptions of TASKS and maneuver tolerances are not included in these standards because this information can be found in the current issue of the listed references, as amended. Publications other than those listed may be used for references if their content conveys substantially the same meaning as the referenced publications.

This PTS is based on the following references:

14 CFR part 61	Certification: Pilots, Flight Instructors, and Ground Instructors
14 CFR part 71	Designation of Class A, B, C, D, and E Airspace Areas; Air Traffic Service Routes, and Reporting Points
14 CFR part 91	General Operating and Flight Rules
14 CFR part 95	IFR Altitudes
14 CFR part 97	Standard Instrument Procedures
AC 61-65	Certification: Pilots and Flight and Ground Instructors
AC 61-98	Currency Requirements and Guidance for the Flight Review and Instrument Proficiency Check
FAA-H-8083-9	Aviation Instructor's Handbook
FAA-H-8083-15	Instrument Flying Handbook
FAA-H-8083-25	Pilot's Handbook of Aeronautical Knowledge
FAA-H-8083-28	Aviation Weather Handbook

FAA-S-ACS-8	Instrument Rating – Airplane Airman Certification Standards
FAA-S-ACS-14	Instrument Rating – Helicopter Airman Certification Standards
AIM	Aeronautical Information Manual
IAP	Instrument Approach Procedures
Other	Aircraft Flight Manual Chart Supplements

NOTE: Users should reference the current edition of the reference documents listed above. The current edition of all FAA publications can be found at: www.faa.gov.

Abbreviations/Acronyms

14 CFR	Title 14 of the Code of Federal Regulations
ACS	Airman Certification Standards
AD	Airworthiness Directive
ADF	Automatic Direction Finder
ADM	Aeronautical Decision-Making
AELS	Aviation English Language Standard
AIM	Aeronautical Information Manual
AIRMET	Airman's Meteorological Information
AKTR	Airman Knowledge Test Report
ASI	Aviation Safety Inspector
ASOS	Automated Surface Observing System
ATC	Air Traffic Control
ATIS	Automatic Terminal Information
AWOS	Automated Weather Observing System
CFIT	Controlled Flight Into Terrain
CRM	Crew Resource Management
DA	Decision Altitude
DH	Decision Height
DME	Distance Measuring Equipment
DP	Departure Procedure
EFB	Electronic Flight Bag
FAA	Federal Aviation Administration
FFS	Full Flight Simulator

FMS	Flight Management System
FSO	Flight Standards Office
FSTD	Flight Simulation Training Device
FTD	Flight Training Device
GFA	Graphical Forecasts for Aviation
GPS	Global Positioning System
IAP	Instrument Approach Procedures
ID	Identification
IFR	Instrument Flight Rules
ILS	Instrument Landing System
IMC	Instrument Meteorological Conditions
LAHSO	Land and Hold Short Operations
LCG	Learner-Centered Grading
MDA	Minimum Descent Altitude
METAR	Aviation Routine Weather Report
MFD	Multi-function Display
NOTAM	Notice to Air Missions
PA	Precision Approach
PDF	Portable Document Format
PIREP	Pilot Report
PTS	Practical Test Standards
RAIM	Receiver Autonomous Integrity Monitoring
RM	Risk Management
RMI	Radio Magnetic Indicator
RNAV	Area Navigation
RNP	Required Navigation Performance
SA	Situational Awareness
SIGMET	Significant Meteorological Advisory
SOP	Standard Operating Procedure
SRM	Single Pilot Resource Management
STAR	Standard Terminal Arrival
TAF	Terminal Area Forecast
TCE	Training Center Evaluator
U.S.	United States of America
VOR	Very High Frequency Omnidirectional Range

Use of the PTS

The FAA requires that all practical tests be conducted in accordance with the appropriate practical test standards.

All of the procedures and maneuvers in the instrument rating practical test standards have been included in the flight instructor instrument practical test standards; however, to permit completion of the practical test for initial certification within a reasonable time-frame, the evaluator shall select one or more TASKS in each AREA OF OPERATION. In certain AREAS OF OPERATION, there are required TASKS that the evaluator must select. These required TASKS are identified by a **NOTE** immediately following each AREA OF OPERATION title.

In preparation for each practical test, the evaluator shall prepare a written "plan of action." The plan of action includes a scenario. The evaluator must develop a scenario that allows the evaluation of most of the AREAS OF OPERATIONS and TASKS required in the practical tests with minimum disruptions. During the scenario, the evaluator interjects problems and emergencies that the applicant must handle. It should be structured so that most of the AREAS OF OPERATIONS and TASKS are accomplished within the scenario. The evaluator must maintain the flexibility to change the scenario due to unexpected situations as they arise and still result in an efficient and valid test. Some tasks (e.g., unusual attitudes) are not normally done during routine flight operations or may not fit into the scenario. These maneuvers still must be demonstrated. It is preferable that these maneuvers be demonstrated after the scenario is completed. But, the practical test scenario can be suspended to do maneuvers and resumed if the situation, due to time and efficiency of the practical test, dictates so. **Any TASK selected for evaluation during a practical test shall be evaluated in its entirety.**

The applicant will use a view-limiting device when performing AREA OF OPERATION VI, TASK H, Recovery from Unusual Attitudes and in AREA OF OPERATION VIII, TASK A, Nonprecision Instrument Approach.

The flight instructor instrument applicant should be prepared in **all** knowledge and skill areas and be prepared to demonstrate the ability to instruct effectively in **all** TASKS included in the AREAS OF OPERATION of this PTS. Throughout the flight portion of the practical test, the evaluator shall evaluate the applicant's ability to demonstrate and simultaneously explain the selected procedures and maneuvers, and to give flight instruction to students at various stages of flight training and levels of experience.

The term "instructional knowledge" means that the flight instructor applicant's discussions, explanations, and descriptions should follow the recommended teaching procedures and techniques explained in FAA-H-8083- 9, Aviation Instructor's Handbook. This includes the development of scenario-based lessons, the ability to evaluate SRM skills, and the ability to use learner-centered grading.

The purpose of including common errors in certain TASKS is to assist the evaluator in determining that the flight instructor applicant has the ability to recognize, analyze, and correct such errors. The evaluator will not simulate any condition that may jeopardize safe flight or result in possible damage to the aircraft. The common errors listed in the TASKS objective may or may not be found in the TASK References. However, the FAA considers their frequency of occurrence justification for inclusion in the TASK Objectives.

Special Emphasis Areas

Evaluators shall place special emphasis upon areas of aircraft operations considered critical to flight safety. Among these are:

1. Positive aircraft control;
2. Positive exchange of the flight controls procedure (who is flying the aircraft);
3. Stall/spin awareness, as applicable;
4. Collision avoidance;
5. Wake turbulence avoidance;
6. LAHSO;
7. Runway incursion avoidance;
8. CFIT;
9. ADM and RM;
10. Checklist usage;
11. SRM;
12. Icing condition operational hazards, anti-icing and deicing equipment, differences, and approved use and operations;
13. RNP;
14. CRM for multi-pilot aircraft; and
15. Other areas deemed appropriate to any phase of the practical test.

With the exception of SRM, any given area may not be addressed specifically under a TASK, but all areas are essential to flight safety and will be evaluated during the practical test.

Aircraft and Equipment Requirements

14 CFR part 61, section 61.45 provides requirements for aircraft and equipment for the practical test.

Use of RNAV or RNP Navigation System

For practical tests conducted in an aircraft equipped with an installed, IFR approved RNAV or RNP system, or in a FSTD equipped to replicate an installed IFR approved RNAV or RNP system, the applicant must demonstrate approach proficiency using that system. The applicant may use a suitable RNAV system on conventional procedures and routes as described in the AIM to accomplish ACS tasks on conventional approach procedures, as appropriate.

Vertical or Lateral Deviation Standard

The standard is to allow no more than a ¾ scale deflection of either the vertical or lateral deviation indications during the final approach. As markings on flight instruments vary, a ¾ scale deflection of either vertical or lateral guidance is deemed to occur when it is displaced three-fourths of the distance that it may be deflected from the indication representing that the aircraft is on the correct flight path.

Nonprecision Approach

A nonprecision approach is a standard instrument approach procedure to a published minimum descent altitude without approved vertical guidance. The applicant may use navigation systems that display advisory vertical guidance during nonprecision approach operations without restriction.

The evaluator must select, and the applicant must accomplish at least two different nonprecision approaches in simulated or actual instrument meteorological conditions:

- At least one procedure must include a course reversal maneuver (e.g., procedure turn, holding in lieu, or the course reversal from an initial approach fix on a Terminal Area Arrival).

- The applicant must accomplish at least one procedure from an initial approach fix without the use of autopilot and without the assistance of radar vectors. During this Task, flying without using the autopilot does not prevent use of the yaw damper and flight director.

- The applicant must fly one procedure with reference to backup or partial panel instrumentation or navigation display, depending on the aircraft's instrument avionics configuration, representing the failure mode(s) most realistic for the equipment used.

The evaluator has discretion to have the applicant perform a landing or a missed approach at the completion of each approach.

Precision Approach

The applicant must accomplish a precision approach to the DA using aircraft navigational equipment for centerline and vertical guidance in simulated or actual instrument meteorological conditions. A precision approach is a standard instrument approach procedure to a published decision altitude using provided approved vertical guidance.

The evaluator has discretion to have the applicant perform a landing or a missed approach at the completion of each approach.

Other Requirements

To assist in management of the aircraft during the practical test, the applicant is expected to demonstrate automation management skills by utilizing installed, available, or airborne equipment such as autopilot, avionics and systems displays, and/or an FMS. The evaluator is expected to test the applicant's knowledge of the systems that are available or installed and operative during both the ground and flight portions of the practical test. If the applicant has trained using a portable EFB to display charts and data and wishes to use the EFB during the practical test, the applicant is expected to demonstrate appropriate knowledge, risk management, and skill appropriate to its use.

If the practical test involves maneuvering the aircraft solely by reference to instruments, the applicant is required by 14 CFR part 61, section 61.45(d)(2) to provide an appropriate view limiting device acceptable to the Administrator. The applicant and the evaluator should establish a procedure as to when and how this device should be donned and removed and brief this procedure before the flight. This device must prevent the applicant from having visual reference outside the aircraft, but it must not restrict the evaluator's ability to see and avoid other traffic. The use of the device does not apply to specific elements within a Task when there is a requirement for visual references.

Use of FAA-Approved FSTD

An airman applicant for instrument rating certification, including a flight instructor instrument rating, is authorized to use an FFS qualified by the National Simulator Program as levels A–D and/or a FTD qualified by the National Simulator Program as levels 4–7 to complete certain flight TASK requirements listed in this practical test standard.

In order to do so, such devices must be used pursuant to and in accordance with a curriculum approved for use at a 14 CFR part 141 pilot school or 14 CFR part 142 training center. Practical tests or portions thereof, when accomplished in an FSTD, may only be conducted by FAA aviation safety inspectors, designees authorized to conduct such tests in FSTDs for part 141 pilot school graduates, or appropriately authorized part 142 TCEs.

When flight TASKS are accomplished in an aircraft, certain TASK elements may be accomplished through "simulated" actions in the interest of safety and practicality, but when accomplished in a flight simulator or flight training device, these same actions would not be "simulated." For example, when in an aircraft, a simulated engine fire may be addressed by retarding the throttle to idle, simulating the shutdown of the engine, simulating the discharge of the fire suppression agent, if applicable, simulating the disconnection of associated electrical, hydraulic, and pneumatics systems. However, when the same emergency condition is addressed in a FSTD, all TASK elements must be accomplished as would be expected under actual circumstances.

Similarly, certain safety of flight precautions taken in the aircraft for the accomplishment of a specific maneuver or procedure (such as limiting altitude in an approach to stall or setting maximum airspeed for an engine failure expected to result in a rejected takeoff) need not be taken when a FSTD is used.

It is important to understand that, whether accomplished in an aircraft or FSTD, all TASKS and elements for each maneuver or procedure shall have the same performance standards applied equally for determination of overall satisfactory performance.

The PTS requires at least one instrument approach procedure be demonstrated in an airplane or helicopter, as appropriate. One precision and one nonprecision approach not selected for actual flight demonstration may be performed in FSTDs that meet the requirements of Appendix 1 of this practical test standard.

Evaluator Responsibility

The evaluator must determine that the applicant meets the AELS. An applicant for an FAA certificate or rating must be able to communicate in English in a discernible and understandable manner with ATC, pilots, and others involved in preparing an aircraft for flight and operating an aircraft in flight. This communication may or may not involve radio communications. An applicant for an FAA certificate issued in accordance with 14 CFR part 61 who cannot hear or speak due to a medical deficiency may be eligible for an FAA certificate with specific operational limitations. For additional information, reference AC 60-28, FAA English

Language Standard for an FAA Certificate Issued Under 14 CFR parts 61, 63, 65, and 107, as amended.

If the applicant's ability to meet the FAA AELS comes into question before starting the practical test, the evaluator will not begin the practical test. An evaluator who is not an ASI[1] will check the box, *Referred to FSO for Aviation English Language Standard Determination*, located on the bottom of page 2 of the applicant's FAA Form 8710-1, Application for an Airman Certificate and/or Rating. The evaluator will refer the applicant to the appropriate FSO. ASIs conducting the practical test may assess an applicant's English language proficiency in accordance with FAA Order 8900.1.

If the applicant's ability to meet the FAA AELS comes into question after the practical test begins, an evaluator who is not an ASI will discontinue the practical test and check the box, *Referred to FSO for Aviation English Language Standard Determination*, on the application. The evaluator will also issue an FAA Form 8060-5, Notice of Disapproval Application, with the comment "Does Not Demonstrate FAA AELS" in addition to any unsatisfactory Task(s).

In either case, the evaluator must complete and submit the application file through normal application procedures and notify the appropriate FSO of the referral.

The evaluator conducting the practical test is responsible for determining that the applicant meets acceptable standards of teaching ability, knowledge, and skill in the selected TASKS. The evaluator makes this determination by accomplishing an Objective that is appropriate to each selected TASK, and includes an evaluation of the applicant's:

1. Ability to apply the fundamentals of instructing;
2. Knowledge of, and ability to teach, the subject matter, procedures, and maneuvers covered in the TASKS;
3. Ability to perform the procedures and maneuvers included in the standards to the INSTRUMENT PILOT skill level while giving effective flight instruction;
4. Ability to analyze and correct common errors related to the procedures and maneuvers covered in the TASKS;
5. Ability to develop scenario-based instruction that meets lesson objectives;
6. Ability to teach and evaluate SRM and CRM, to include multi-pilot aircraft; and

---

[1] ASIs may assess an applicant's English language proficiency in accordance with FAA Order 8900.1.

7. Ability to use learner-centered grading and debriefing techniques appropriately.

It is intended that oral questioning be used at any time during the ground or flight portion of the practical test to determine that the applicant can instruct effectively and has a comprehensive knowledge of the TASKS and their related safety factors. Oral questioning, should be used judiciously at all times, especially during the flight portion of the practical test.

Evaluators should, to the greatest extent possible, test the applicant's application and correlation skills. When possible, scenario based questions should be used.

During the flight portion of the practical test, the evaluator shall act as a student during selected maneuvers. This will give the evaluator an opportunity to evaluate the flight instructor applicant's ability to analyze and correct simulated common errors related to these maneuvers. The evaluator will also evaluate the applicant's use of visual scanning and collision avoidance procedures, and the applicant's ability to teach those procedures.

If the evaluator determines that a Task is incomplete, or the outcome uncertain, the evaluator will require the applicant to repeat that Task, or portions of that Task. This provision has been made in the interest of fairness and does not mean that instruction, practice, or the repeating of an unsatisfactory task is permitted during the certification process.

The evaluator shall place special emphasis on the applicant's demonstrated ability to teach precise aircraft control and sound judgment in aeronautical decision-making. Evaluation of the applicant's ability to teach judgment shall be accomplished by asking the applicant to describe the oral discussions and the presentation of practical problems that would be used in instructing students in the exercise of sound judgment. The evaluator shall also emphasize the evaluation of the applicant's demonstrated ability to teach spatial disorientation, wake turbulence and low-level wind shear avoidance, checklist usage, positive exchange of flight controls, and any other directed special emphasis areas.

Flight Instructor Responsibility

An appropriately rated flight instructor is responsible for training the flight instructor applicant to acceptable standards in all subject matter areas, procedures, and maneuvers included in the TASKS within each AREA OF OPERATION in the appropriate flight instructor practical test standard.

Because of the impact of their teaching activities in developing safe, proficient pilots, flight instructors should exhibit a high level of knowledge, skill, and the ability to impart that knowledge and skill to students. The flight instructor shall certify that the applicant is:

1. Able to make a practical application of the fundamentals of instructing;
2. Competent to teach the subject matter, procedures, and maneuvers included in the standards to students with varying backgrounds and levels of experience and ability;
3. Able to perform the procedures and maneuvers included in the standards to the INSTRUMENT PILOT skill level while giving effective flight instruction; and
4. Competent to pass the required practical test for the issuance of the flight instructor instrument certificate with the associated category and class ratings or the addition of a category and/or class rating to a flight instructor instrument certificate.

Satisfactory Performance

14 CFR part 61, section 61.43(a), describes satisfactory completion of the practical test for a certificate or rating.

The practical test is passed if, in the judgment of the evaluator, the applicant demonstrates satisfactory performance with regard to:

1. Knowledge of the fundamentals of instructing;
2. Knowledge of the technical subject areas;
3. Knowledge of the flight instructor's responsibilities concerning the pilot certification process;
4. Knowledge of the flight instructor's responsibilities concerning logbook entries and pilot certificate endorsements;
5. Ability to demonstrate the procedures and maneuvers selected by the evaluator to the instrument instructor pilot skill level while giving effective instruction;
6. Competence in teaching the procedures and maneuvers selected by the evaluator;
7. Competence in describing, recognizing, analyzing, and correcting common errors simulated by the evaluator; and
8. Knowledge of the development and effective use of a course of training, a syllabus, and a lesson plan, including scenario-based training and collaborative assessment.

Unsatisfactory Performance

If, in the judgment of the evaluator, the applicant does not meet the standards of performance of any Task performed, the associated Area of Operation is failed and, therefore, the practical test is failed. 14 CFR part 61, section 61.43(c)-(f) provides additional unsatisfactory performance requirements and parameters.

Typical reasons for unsatisfactory and grounds for disqualification are:

1. Failure to perform a procedure or maneuver to the instrument pilot skill level while giving effective flight instruction;
2. Failure to provide an effective instructional explanation while demonstrating a procedure or maneuver (explanation during the demonstration must be clear, concise, technically accurate, and complete with no prompting from the evaluator);
3. Any action or lack of action by the applicant which requires corrective intervention by the evaluator to maintain safe flight;
4. Failure to use proper and effective visual scanning techniques to clear the area before and while performing maneuvers; and
5. Failure to incorporate SRM principles throughout the practical test.

When a notice of disapproval is issued, the evaluator shall record the applicant's unsatisfactory performance in terms of AREAS OF OPERATION.

Letter of Discontinuance

When a practical test is discontinued for reasons other than unsatisfactory performance (e.g., equipment failure, weather, or illness) FAA Form 8710-1, Airman Certificate and/or Rating Application, and, if applicable, the Airman Knowledge Test Report, shall be returned to the applicant. The evaluator at that time shall prepare, sign, and issue a Letter of Discontinuance to the applicant. The Letter of Discontinuance should identify the AREAS OF OPERATION of the practical test that were successfully completed. The applicant shall be advised that the Letter of Discontinuance shall be presented to the evaluator when the practical test is resumed, and made part of the certification file.

ADM, Risk Management, CRM, and SRM

Throughout the practical test, the evaluator must assess the applicant's ability to use sound aeronautical decision-making procedures in order to identify hazards and mitigate risk. The evaluator must accomplish this requirement by developing scenarios that incorporate and combine

Tasks appropriate to assessing the applicant's risk management in making safe aeronautical decisions. For example, the evaluator may develop a scenario that incorporates weather decisions and performance planning.

In assessing the applicant's performance, the evaluator should take note of the applicant's use of CRM and, if appropriate, SRM. CRM/SRM are the set of competencies that includes situational awareness, communication skills, teamwork, task allocation, and decision-making within a comprehensive framework of SOP. SRM specifically refers to the management of all resources onboard the aircraft, as well as outside resources available to the single pilot.

If an applicant fails to use ADM, including CRM/SRM, as applicable in any Task, the evaluator will note that Task as failed.

Applicant's Use of Checklists

Throughout the practical test, the applicant is evaluated on the use of an appropriate checklist. Proper use is dependent on the specific TASK being evaluated. The situation may be such that the use of the checklist, while accomplishing elements of an Objective, would be either unsafe or impracticable, especially in a single-pilot operation. In this case, a review of the checklist after the elements have been accomplished would be appropriate. Division of attention and proper visual scanning should be considered when using a checklist.

Use of Distractions During Practical Tests

Numerous studies indicate that many accidents have occurred when the pilot has been distracted during critical phases of flight. To evaluate the pilot's ability to utilize proper control technique while dividing attention both inside and/or outside the flight deck, the evaluator shall cause a realistic distraction during the flight portion of the practical test to evaluate the applicant's ability to divide attention while maintaining safe flight.

Positive Exchange of Flight Controls

During flight, there must always be a clear understanding between pilots of who has control of the aircraft. Prior to flight, a briefing should be conducted that includes the procedure for the exchange of flight controls. A positive three-step process, subsequently described, in the exchange of flight controls between pilots is a proven procedure and one that is strongly recommended.

When one pilot wishes to give the other pilot control of the aircraft, they will say, "You have the flight controls." The other pilot acknowledges immediately by saying, "I have the flight controls." The first pilot again says, "You have the flight controls." When control is returned to the first pilot, follow the same procedure. A visual check is recommended to verify that the exchange has occurred. There should never be any doubt as to who is flying the aircraft.

Emphasis on Attitude Instrument Flying and Partial Panel Skills

The FAA is concerned about numerous fatal accidents involving spatial disorientation of instrument rated pilots who have attempted to control and maneuver their aircraft in clouds with inoperative primary flight instruments (gyroscopic heading and/or attitude indicators) or loss of the primary electric flight instruments display.

The FAA has stressed that it is imperative for instrument pilots to acquire and maintain adequate instrument skills and that they be capable of performing instrument flight with the use of the backup systems installed in the aircraft. Many light aircraft operated in IMC are not equipped with dual, independent gyroscopic heading and/or attitude indicators and in many cases are equipped with only a single vacuum source. Technically advanced aircraft may be equipped with backup flight instruments or an additional electronic flight display that is not located directly in front of the pilot.

FAA-S-ACS-8, Instrument Rating – Airplane Airman Certification Standards and FAA-S-8081-9, Flight Instructor—Instrument Practical Test Standards, place increased emphasis on and require the demonstration of a nonprecision instrument approach without the use of the primary flight instruments or electronic flight instrument display. This practical test book, FAA-S-8081-9, emphasizes this area from an instructional standpoint.

AREA OF OPERATION VI requires the applicant to demonstrate the ability to teach basic instrument flight TASKS under both full panel and reference to backup primary flight instruments/electronic flight instrument displays. These maneuvers are described in detail in FAA-H-8083-15, Instrument Flying Handbook. Evaluators should determine that the applicant demonstrates and fully understands either the PRIMARY and SUPPORTING or the CONTROL and PERFORMANCE CONCEPT method of attitude instrument flying. Both attitude instrument flying methods are described in FAA-H-8083-15, Instrument Flying Handbook. The TASKS require the applicant to exhibit instructional knowledge of instrument flying techniques and procedures and to demonstrate the ability to teach basic instrument maneuvers with both full panel and partial panel or reference to backup primary flight instruments/electronic flight instrument displays.

Addition of an Instrument Instructor Rating to a Flight Instructor Certificate

AREA OF OPERATION	FLIGHT INSTRUCTOR CERTIFICATE AND RATING HELD					
	AP	RTR	PL	IA	IH	IP
I	N	N	N	N	N	N
II	A & C	A & C	A & C	C	C	C
III	B & C	B & C	B & C	C	C	C
IV	N	N	N	N	N	N
V	Y	Y	Y	N	N	N
VI	Y	Y	Y	Y	Y	Y
VII	Y	Y	Y	N	N	N
VIII	Y	Y	Y	*A or B	*A or B	*A or B
IX	Y	Y	Y	Y	Y	Y
X	Y	Y	Y	Y	Y	Y

LEGEND
AP—Airplane
RTR—Helicopter
PL—Powered-Lift
IA—Instrument Airplane
IH—Instrument Helicopter
IP—Instrument Powered-Lift

NOTE: N indicates that the AREA OF OPERATION is not required. Y indicates that the AREA OF OPERATION is to be performed or based on the NOTE in the AREA OF OPERATION. If a TASK (or TASKS) is listed for an AREA OF OPERATION, that TASK (or TASKS) is mandatory.

*Combine with C, D, or E.

Renewal or Reinstatement of a Flight Instructor

REQUIRED AREAS OF OPERATION	NUMBER OF TASKS
II	TASK "D" and one other TASK
III	1
IV	1
V	1
VI	2
VII	1
VIII	A or B combined with TASK C, D, or E
IX	1

The renewal or reinstatement of one rating on a Flight Instructor Certificate renews or reinstates all privileges existing on the certificate. (14 CFR part 61, sections 61.197 and 61.199)

Applicant's Practical Test Checklist
Flight Instructor—Instrument

Appointment with Evaluator: _____

Name _____

Date/Time _____

- ☐ View-limiting Device
- ☐ Aircraft Documents:
    - ☐ Airworthiness Certificate
    - ☐ Registration Certificate
    - ☐ Operating Limitations
- ☐ Aircraft Maintenance Records:
    - ☐ Logbook Record of Airworthiness Inspections and AD Compliance
- ☐ Pilot's Operating Handbook and FAA-Approved Flight Manual

PERSONAL EQUIPMENT

- ☐ PTS Lesson Plan
- ☐ Current Aeronautical Charts
- ☐ Computer and Plotter
- ☐ Flight Plan and Flight Log Forms
- ☐ Current AIM
- ☐ Chart Supplements
- ☐ Appropriate Publications

PERSONAL RECORDS

- ☐ Identification—Photo/Signature ID
- ☐ Pilot Certificate
- ☐ Current and Appropriate Medical Certificate
- ☐ Completed FAA Form 8710-1, Airman Certificate and/or Rating Application
- ☐ AKTR
- ☐ Pilot Logbook with Appropriate Instructor Endorsements
- ☐ FAA Form 8060-5, Notice of Disapproval Application (if applicable)
- ☐ Letter of Discontinuance (if applicable)
- ☐ Approved School Graduation Certificate (if applicable)
- ☐ Evaluator's Fee (if applicable)

Evaluator's Practical Test Checklist
Flight Instructor—Instrument

Applicant's Name _____

Location _____

Date/Time _____

I. FUNDAMENTALS OF INSTRUCTING

A. The Learning Process
B. Human Behavior and Effective Communication
C. The Teaching Process
D. Teaching Methods
E. Critique and Evaluation
F. Flight Instructor Characteristics and Responsibilities
G. Planning Instructional Activity

II. TECHNICAL SUBJECT AREAS

A. Aircraft Flight Instruments and Navigation Equipment
B. Aeromedical Factors
C. Regulations and Publications Related to IFR Operations
D. Logbook Entries Related to Instrument Instruction

III. PREFLIGHT PREPARATION

A. Weather Information
B. Cross-Country Flight Planning
C. Instrument Flight Deck Check

IV. PREFLIGHT LESSON ON A MANEUVER TO BE PERFORMED IN FLIGHT

A. Maneuver Lesson

V. ATC CLEARANCES AND PROCEDURES

A. ATC Clearances
B. Compliance with Departure, En Route, and Arrival Procedures and Clearances

VI. FLIGHT BY REFERENCE TO INSTRUMENTS

A. Straight-and-Level Flight
B. Turns
C. Change of Airspeed in Straight-and-Level and Turning Flight

D. Constant Airspeed Climbs and Descents
E. Constant Rate Climbs and Descents
F. Timed Turns to Magnetic Compass Headings
G. Steep Turns
H. Recovery from Unusual Flight Attitudes

VII. NAVIGATION AIDS

A. Intercepting and Tracking Navigational Systems and DME Arcs
B. Holding Procedures

VIII. INSTRUMENT APPROACH PROCEDURES

A. Nonpecision Instrument Approach
B. Precision Instrument Approach
C. Missed Approach
D. Circling Approach (Airplane)
E. Landing From a Straight-In Approach

IX. EMERGENCY OPERATIONS

A. Loss of Communications
B. Approach with Loss of Primary Instrument Indicators
C. Engine Failure During Straight-and-Level Flight and Turns (Multiengine)
D. Instrument Approach—One Engine Inoperative (Multiengine)

X. POSTFLIGHT PROCEDURES

A. Checking Instruments and Equipment

I. AREA OF OPERATION: FUNDAMENTALS OF INSTRUCTING

NOTE: The evaluator shall select at least TASK E, F, and G and one other task.

A. TASK: LEARNING PROCESS

REFERENCE: FAA-H-8083-9.

Objective. To determine that the applicant exhibits instructional knowledge of the elements of the learning process by describing:

1. Learning theories.
2. Characteristics of learning.
3. Principles of learning.
4. Levels of learning.
5. Learning physical skills.
6. Memory.
7. Transfer of learning.

B. TASK: HUMAN BEHAVIOR AND EFFECTIVE COMMUNICATION

REFERENCE: FAA-H-8083-9.

Objective. To determine that the applicant exhibits instructional knowledge of the elements of human behavior and effective communication as it applies to the teaching/learning process by describing:

1. Human behavior—
   a. control of human behavior.
   b. human needs.
   c. defense mechanisms.
   d. the flight instructor as a practical psychologist.
2. Effective communication
   a. basic elements of communication.
   b. barriers of effective communication.
   c. developing communication skills.

C. TASK: TEACHING PROCESS

REFERENCE: FAA-H-8083-9.

Objective. To determine that the applicant exhibits instructional knowledge of the elements of the teaching process by describing:

1. Preparation of a lesson for a ground or flight instructional period.
2. Presentation methods.
3. Application, by the student, of the material or procedure that was presented.
4. Review and evaluation of student performance.
5. Problem-based learning.

D. TASK: TEACHING METHODS

REFERENCE: FAA-H-8083-9.

Objective. To determine that the applicant exhibits instructional knowledge of the elements of teaching methods by describing:

1. Material organization.
2. The lecture method.
3. The cooperative or group learning method.
4. The guided discussion method.
5. The demonstration-performance method.
6. Computer-based training method.
7. Scenario-based training method.

E. TASK: CRITIQUE AND EVALUATION

REFERENCE: FAA-H-8083-9.

Objective. To determine that the applicant exhibits instructional knowledge of the elements of critique and evaluation by explaining:

1. Critique—

   a. purpose and characteristics of an effective critique.
   b. methods and ground rules for a critique.

2. Evaluation—

   a. characteristics of effective oral questions and what types to avoid.
   b. responses to student questions.
   c. characteristics and development of effective written test.
   d. characteristics and uses of performance tests, specifically, the FAA PTS.
   e. collaborative assessment (or LCG).

F. TASK: FLIGHT INSTRUCTOR CHARACTERISTICS AND RESPONSIBILITIES

REFERENCE: FAA-H-8083-9.

Objective. To determine that the applicant exhibits instructional knowledge of the elements of instructor responsibilities and professionalism by describing:

1. Aviation instructor responsibilities in—
   a. providing adequate instruction.
   b. establishing standards of performance.
   c. emphasizing the positive.

2. Flight instructor responsibilities in—
   a. providing student pilot evaluation and supervision.
   b. preparing practical test recommendations and endorsements.
   c. determining requirements for conducting additional training and endorsement requirements.

3. Professionalism as an instructor by—
   a. explaining important personal characteristics.
   b. describing methods to minimize student frustration.

G. TASK: PLANNING INSTRUCTIONAL ACTIVITY

REFERENCE: FAA-H-8083-9.

Objective. To determine that the applicant exhibits instructional knowledge of the elements of planning instructional activity by describing:

1. Developing objectives and standards for a course of training.
2. Theory of building blocks of learning.
3. Requirements for developing a training syllabus.
4. Purpose and characteristics of a lesson plan.
5. How a scenario-based lesson is developed.

II. AREA OF OPERATION: TECHNICAL SUBJECT AREAS

NOTE: The evaluator shall select TASKS A and D and at least one other TASK.

A. TASK: AIRCRAFT FLIGHT INSTRUMENTS AND NAVIGATION EQUIPMENT

REFERENCES: FAA-H-8083-15; FAA-S-ACS-8, FAA-S-ACS-14.

Objective. To determine that the applicant exhibits instructional knowledge of aircraft:

1. Flight instrument systems and their operating characteristics to include—
   a. pitot-static system.
   b. attitude indicator.
   c. heading indicator/horizontal situation indicator/radio magnetic indicator.
   d. magnetic compass.
   e. turn-and-slip indicator/turn coordinator.
   f. electrical system.
   g. vacuum system.
   h. electronic engine instrument display.
   i. primary flight display, if installed.

2. Navigation equipment and their operating characteristics to include—
   a. VHF omnirange (VOR).
   b. DME.
   c. ILS
   d. marker beacon receiver/indicators.
   e. ADF.
   f. transponder/altitude encoding.
   g. electronic flight instrument display.
   h. GPS.
   i. automatic pilot.
   j. FMS.
   k. multifunction display, if installed.

3. Anti-ice/deicing and weather detection equipment and their operating characteristics to include—
   a. airframe.
   b. propeller or rotor.
   c. air intake.
   d. fuel system.

e. pitot-static system.
f. radar/lightning detection system.
g. other inflight weather systems.

B. TASK: AEROMEDICAL FACTORS

REFERENCES: FAA-H-8083-25; AIM.

Objective. To determine that the applicant exhibits instructional knowledge of the elements related to aeromedical factors by describing the effects, corrective action, and safety considerations of:

1. Hypoxia.
2. Hyperventilation.
3. Middle ear and sinus problems.
4. Spatial disorientation.
5. Motion sickness.
6. Alcohol and drugs.
7. Carbon monoxide poisoning.
8. Evolved gases from scuba diving.
9. Stress and fatigue.

C. TASK: REGULATIONS AND PUBLICATIONS RELATED TO IFR OPERATIONS

REFERENCES: 14 CFR parts 61, 71, 91, 95, and 97; FAA-H-8083-15; AIM.

Objective. To determine that the applicant exhibits instructional knowledge of the elements related to regulations and publications, (related to instrument flight and instrument flight instruction) their purpose, general content, availability, and method of revision by describing:

1. 14 CFR parts 61, 71, 91, 95, and 97.
2. FAA-H-8083-15, Instrument Flying Handbook.
3. Aeronautical Information Manual.
4. Practical Test Standards.
5. Chart Supplement.
6. Standard Instrument Departures/Terminal Arrivals.
7. En Route Charts.
8. Standard Instrument Approach Procedure Charts.

D. TASK: LOGBOOK ENTRIES RELATED TO INSTRUMENT INSTRUCTION

REFERENCES: 14 CFR part 61; AC 61-65; AC 61-98.

Objective. To determine that the applicant exhibits instructional knowledge of logbook entries related to instrument instruction by describing:

1. Logbook entries or training records for instrument flight/ instrument flight instruction or ground instruction given.
2. Preparation of a recommendation for an instrument rating practical test, including appropriate logbook entry.
3. Required endorsement of a pilot logbook for satisfactory completion of an instrument proficiency check.
4. Required flight instructor records.

III. AREA OF OPERATION: PREFLIGHT PREPARATION

NOTE: The evaluator shall select at least one TASK.

A. TASK: WEATHER INFORMATION

NOTE: If the current weather reports, forecasts, or other pertinent information is not available, or if the current weather is not appropriate for the practical test scenario, then weather reports, forecasts, and other pertinent information shall be simulated by the evaluator in a manner to adequately measure the applicant's competence.

REFERENCES: FAA-S-ACS-8, FAA-S-ACS-14; FAA-S-8083-28; AIM.

Objective. To determine that the applicant exhibits instructional knowledge related to IFR weather information.

1. Sources of weather—
   a. AWOS, ASOS, and ATIS reports.
   b. Sources of weather data (e.g., National Weather Service, Flight Service) for flight planning purposes.
2. Weather reports and charts—
   a. METAR, TAF, and Graphical Forecasts for Aviation (GFA).
   b. inflight weather advisories.
   c. surface analysis, weather depiction, and radar summary charts.
   d. significant weather prognostic charts.
   e. winds and temperatures aloft charts.
   f. PIREPS.
   g. freezing level charts.
   h. severe weather outlook charts.
   i. SIGMETs and AIRMETs.

B. TASK: CROSS-COUNTRY FLIGHT PLANNING

REFERENCES: 14 CFR part 91; FAA-H-8083-15; FAA-S-ACS-8, FAA-S-ACS-14; AIM.

Objective. To determine that the applicant exhibits instructional knowledge of cross-country flight planning by describing the:

1. Regulatory requirements for instrument flight within various types of airspace.
2. Computation of estimated time en route and total fuel requirement for an IFR cross-country flight.

3. Selection and correct interpretation of the current and applicable en route charts, RNAV, DPs, STARs, and standard IAP.
4. Procurement and interpretation of the applicable NOTAM information.
5. Completes and files an IFR flight plan that accurately reflects the conditions of the proposed flight. (Does not have to be filed with ATC.)
6. Demonstrates adequate knowledge of GPS and RAIM capability, when aircraft is so equipped.
7. Demonstrates the ability to recognize wing contamination due to airframe icing.
8. Demonstrates adequate knowledge of the adverse effects of airframe icing during landing phases of flight and corrective actions: pretakeoff, takeoff, and cruise.
9. Demonstrates familiarity with any icing procedures and/or information published by the manufacturer that is specific to the aircraft used on the practical test.

C. TASK: INSTRUMENT FLIGHT DECK CHECK

REFERENCES: 14 CFR part 91; FAA-H-8083-15; FAA-S-ACS-8, FAA-S-ACS-14.

Objective. To determine that the applicant exhibits instructional knowledge of an instrument flight deck check by describing the reasons for the check and the detection of defects that could affect safe instrument flight. The check shall include:

1. Communications equipment.
2. Navigation equipment.
3. Magnetic compass.
4. Heading indicator/horizontal situation indicator/remote magnetic indicator.
5. Attitude indicator.
6. Altimeter.
7. Turn-and-slip indicator/turn coordinator.
8. Vertical-speed indicator.
9. Airspeed indicator.
10. Outside air temperature.
11. Clock.
12. Pitot heat.
13. Electronic flight instrument display.
14. Traffic awareness/warning/avoidance system.
15. Terrain awareness/warning/alert system.
16. FMS.
17. Automatic pilot.

IV. AREA OF OPERATION: PREFLIGHT LESSON ON A MANEUVER TO BE PERFORMED IN FLIGHT

NOTE: The evaluator shall select at least one maneuver from AREAS OF OPERATION VI through IX and ask the applicant to present a preflight lesson on the selected maneuver as the lesson would be taught to a student. Previously developed lesson plans from the applicant's library may be used.

A. TASK: MANEUVER LESSON

REFERENCES: FAA-H-8083-9, FAA-H-8083-15; FAA-S-ACS-8, FAA-S-ACS-14.

Objective. To determine that the applicant exhibits instructional knowledge of the selected maneuver by:

1. Using a lesson plan that includes all essential items to make an effective and organized presentation.
2. Stating the objective.
3. Giving an accurate, comprehensive oral description of the maneuver, including the elements and associated common errors.
4. Using instructional aids, as appropriate.
5. Describing the recognition, analysis, and correction of common errors.

V. AREA OF OPERATION: AIR TRAFFIC CONTROL CLEARANCES AND PROCEDURES

NOTE: The evaluator shall select at least one TASK.

A. TASK: AIR TRAFFIC CONTROL CLEARANCES

REFERENCES: 14 CFR part 91; FAA-H-8083-15; FAA-S-ACS-8, FAA-S-ACS-14.

Objective. To determine that the applicant exhibits instructional knowledge of air traffic control clearances by describing:

1. Pilot and controller responsibilities to include tower, en route control, and clearance void times.
2. Correct and timely copying of an ATC clearance.
3. Ability to comply with the clearance.
4. Correct and timely read-back of an ATC clearance, using standard phraseology.
5. Correct interpretation of an ATC clearance and, when necessary, request for clarification, verification, or change.
6. Setting of communication and navigation frequencies in compliance with an ATC clearance.

B. TASK: COMPLIANCE WITH DEPARTURE, EN ROUTE, AND ARRIVAL PROCEDURES AND CLEARANCES

REFERENCES: 14 CFR part 91; FAA-H-8083-15; FAA-S-ACS-8, FAA-S-ACS-14; AIM.

Objective. To determine that the applicant exhibits instructional knowledge of the elements related to compliance with departure, en route, and arrival procedures and clearances by describing:

1. Selection and use of current and appropriate navigation publications.
2. Pilot and controller responsibilities with regard to DPs, En Route Low and High Altitude Charts, and STARs.
3. Selection and use of appropriate communications frequencies.
4. Selection and identification of the navigation aids.
5. Accomplishment of the appropriate checklist items.
6. Pilot's responsibility for compliance with vectors and also altitude, airspeed, climb, descent, and airspace restrictions.
7. Pilot's responsibility for the interception of courses, radials, and bearings appropriate to the procedure, route, or clearance.

8. Procedures to be used in the event of two-way communications failure.
9. The uses of the multifunction display and other graphical navigational displays, if installed, to monitor position track, wind drift, and other parameters to maintain situational awareness and desired flightpath.

VI. AREA OF OPERATION: FLIGHT BY REFERENCE TO INSTRUMENTS

NOTE: The evaluator shall select TASK H and at least one other TASK. The applicant shall select either the primary and supporting or the control and performance method for teaching this AREA OF OPERATION.

A. TASK: STRAIGHT-AND-LEVEL FLIGHT

REFERENCES: FAA-H-8083-9, FAA-H-8083-15; FAA-S-ACS-8, FAA-S-ACS-14.

Objective. To determine that the applicant:

1. Exhibits instructional knowledge of teaching straight-and-level flight by describing—

   a. the relationship of pitch, bank, and power in straight-and-level flight.
   b. procedure using full panel and partial panel
   c. coordination of controls and trim.

2. Exhibits instructional knowledge of common errors related to straight-and-level flight by describing—

   a. slow or improper cross-check during straight-and-level flight.
   b. improper power control.
   c. failure to make smooth, precise corrections, as required.
   d. uncoordinated use of controls.
   e. improper trim control.

3. Demonstrates and simultaneously explains straight-and-level flight from an instructional standpoint.
4. Analyzes and corrects simulated common errors related to straight-and-level flight.

B. TASK: TURNS

REFERENCES: FAA-H-8083-9, FAA-H-8083-15; FAA-S-ACS-8, FAA-S-ACS-14.

Objective. To determine that the applicant:

1. Exhibits instructional knowledge of teaching turns by describing—

   a. the relationship of true airspeed and angle of bank to a standard rate turn.

b. technique and procedure using full panel and partial panel for entry and recovery of a constant rate turn, including the performance of a half-standard rate turn.

c. coordination of controls and trim.

2. Exhibits instructional knowledge of common errors related to turns by describing—

a. improper cross-check procedures.

b. improper bank control during roll-in and roll-out.

c. failure to make smooth, precise corrections, as required.

d. uncoordinated use of controls.

e. improper trim technique.

3. Demonstrates and simultaneously explains turns from an instructional standpoint.

4. Analyzes and corrects simulated common errors related to turns.

C. TASK: CHANGE OF AIRPSEED IN STRAIGHT-AND-LEVEL AND TURNING FLIGHT

REFERENCES: FAA-H-8083-9, FAA-H-8083-15; FAA-S-ACS-8, FAA-S-ACS-14.

Objective. To determine that the applicant:

1. Exhibits instructional knowledge of teaching change of airspeed in straight-and-level flight and turns by describing—

a. procedure using full panel and partial panel for maintaining altitude and changing airspeed in straight-and-level and turning flight.

b. coordination of controls and trim technique.

2. Exhibits instructional knowledge of common errors related to changes of airspeed in straight-and- level and turning flight by describing—

a. slow or improper cross-check during straight-and-level flight and turns.

b. improper power control.

c. failure to make smooth, precise corrections, as required.

d. uncoordinated use of controls.

e. improper trim technique.

3. Demonstrates and simultaneously explains changes of airspeed in straight-and-level and turning flight from an instructional standpoint.

4. Analyzes and corrects simulated common errors related to changes of airspeed in straight-and- level and turning flight.

D. TASK: CONSTANT AIRSPEED CLIMBS AND DESCENTS

REFERENCES: FAA-H-8083-9, FAA-H-8083-15; FAA-S-ACS-8, FAA-S-ACS-14.

Objective. To determine that the applicant:

1. Exhibits instructional knowledge of constant airspeed climbs and descents by describing—
   a. procedure using full panel and partial panel for an entry into a straight climb or climbing turn, from either cruising or climbing airspeed.
   b. a stabilized straight climb or climbing turn.
   c. a level-off from a straight climb or climbing turn, at either cruising or climbing airspeed.
   d. procedure using full panel and partial panel for an entry into a straight descent or descending turn from either cruising or descending airspeed.
   e. a stabilized straight descent or descending turn.
   f. a level-off from a straight descent or descending turn, at either cruising or descending airspeed.

2. Exhibits instructional knowledge of common errors related to constant airspeed climbs and descents by describing—
   a. failure to use a proper power setting and pitch attitude.
   b. improper correction of vertical rate, airspeed, heading, or rate-of-turn errors.
   c. uncoordinated use of controls.
   d. improper trim control.

3. Demonstrates and simultaneously explains a constant airspeed climb and a constant airspeed descent from an instructional standpoint.

4. Analyzes and corrects simulated common errors related to constant airspeed climbs and descents.

E. TASK: CONSTANT RATE CLIMBS AND DESCENTS

REFERENCES: FAA-H-8083-9, FAA-H-8083-15; FAA-S-ACS-8, FAA-S-ACS-14.

Objective. To determine that the applicant:

1. Exhibits instructional knowledge of constant rate climbs and descents by describing—

a. procedure using full panel and partial panel for an entry into a constant rate climb or descent.

b. a stabilized constant rate straight climb or climbing turn, using the vertical speed indicator.

c. a level-off from a constant rate straight climb or climbing turn.

d. an entry into a constant rate straight descent or descending turn.

e. a stabilized constant rate straight descent or descending turn using the vertical speed indicator.

f. level-off from a constant rate straight descent or descending turn.

2. Exhibits instructional knowledge of common errors related to constant rate climbs and descents by describing—

a. failure to use a proper power setting and pitch attitude.

b. improper correction of vertical rate, airspeed, heading, or rate-of-turn errors.

c. uncoordinated use of controls.

d. improper trim control.

3. Demonstrates and simultaneously explains a constant rate climb and a constant rate descent from an instructional standpoint.

4. Analyzes and corrects simulated common errors related to constant rate climbs and descents.

F. TASK: TIMED TURNS TO MAGNETIC COMPASS HEADINGS

REFERENCES: FAA-H-8083-9, FAA-H-8083-15; FAA-S-ACS-8, FAA-S-ACS-14.

Objective. To determine that the applicant:

1. Exhibits instructional knowledge of timed turns to magnetic compass headings by describing—

a. operating characteristics and errors of the magnetic compass.

b. calibration of the miniature aircraft of the turn coordinator[1], both right and left, using full panel and the clock.

c. procedures using full panel and partial panel performing compass turns to a specified heading.

---

[1] If the aircraft used for the practical test has a turn needle, substitute turn needle for miniature aircraft of turn coordinator.

2. Exhibits instructional knowledge of common errors related to timed turns to magnetic compass headings by describing—
    a. incorrect calibration procedures.
    b. improper timing.
    c. uncoordinated use of controls.
    d. improper trim control.
3. Demonstrates and simultaneously explains timed turns to magnetic compass headings from an instructional standpoint.
4. Analyzes and corrects simulated common errors related to timed turns to magnetic compass headings.

G. TASK: STEEP TURNS

REFERENCES: FAA-H-8083-9, FAA-H-8083-15; FAA-S-ACS-8, FAA-S-ACS-14.

Objective. To determine that the applicant:

1. Exhibits instructional knowledge of steep turns by describing—
    a. procedure using full panel and partial panel for entry and recovery of a steep turn.
    b. the need for a proper instrument cross-check.
    c. roll-in/roll-out procedure.
    d. coordination of control and trim.
2. Exhibits instructional knowledge of common errors related to steep turns by describing—
    a. failure to recognize and make proper corrections for pitch, bank, or power errors.
    b. failure to compensate for precession of the horizon bar of the attitude indicator.
    c. uncoordinated use of controls.
    d. improper trim technique.
3. Demonstrates and simultaneously explains steep turns from an instructional standpoint.
4. Analyzes and corrects simulated common errors related to steep turns.

H. TASK: RECOVERY FROM UNUSUAL FLIGHT ATTITUDES

REFERENCES: FAA-H-8083-9, FAA-H-8083-15; FAA-S-ACS-8, FAA-S-ACS-14.

Objective. To determine that the applicant:

1. Exhibits instructional knowledge of recovery from unusual flight attitudes by describing—

    a. conditions or situations which contribute to the development of unusual flight attitudes.

    b. procedure using full panel and partial panel for recovery from nose-high and nose-low unusual flight attitudes.

2. Exhibits instructional knowledge of common errors related to recovery from unusual flight attitudes by describing—

    a. incorrect interpretation of the flight instruments.

    b. inappropriate application of controls.

3. Demonstrates and simultaneously explains recovery from unusual flight attitudes, solely by reference to instruments, from an instructional standpoint.

4. Analyzes and corrects simulated common errors related to recovery from unusual flight attitudes.

VII. AREA OF OPERATION: NAVIGATION AIDS

NOTE: The evaluator shall select TASK A and B. If aircraft is not DME equipped, performance of DME arcs shall be tested orally.

A. TASK: INTERCEPTING AND TRACKING NAVIGATIONAL SYSTEMS AND DME ARCS

REFERENCES: 14 CFR part 91; FAA-H-8083-9, FAA-H-8083-15; FAA-S-ACS-8, FAA-S-ACS-14; AIM.

NOTE: While the applicant is expected to be able to fly DME arcs, they may be selected for testing only if they are charted and available (including use of RNAV substitution techniques, if appropriate.)

Objective. To determine that the applicant:

1. Exhibits instructional knowledge of the elements of intercepting and tracking navigational systems and DME arcs by describing—

   a. tuning and identification of a navigational facility.

   b. setting of a selected course on the navigation selector or the correct identification of a selected bearing on the RMI.

   c. method for determining aircraft position relative to a facility.

   d. procedure for intercepting and maintaining a selected course.

   e. procedure for intercepting and maintaining a DME arc.

   f. procedure for intercepting a course or localizer from a DME arc.

   g. recognition of navigation facility or waypoint passage.

   h. recognition of navigation receiver or facility failure.

2. Exhibits instructional knowledge of common errors related to intercepting and tracking navigational systems and DME arcs by describing—

   a. incorrect tuning and identification procedures.

   b. failure to properly set the navigation selector on the course to be intercepted.

   c. failure to use proper procedures for course or DME arc interception and tracking.

   d. improper procedures for intercepting a course or localizer from a DME arc.

3. Demonstrates and simultaneously explains intercepting and tracking navigational systems and DME arcs from an instructional standpoint.

4. Analyzes and corrects simulated common errors related to intercepting and tracking navigational systems and DME arcs.

5. Exhibits instructional knowledge on the uses of the MFD and other graphical navigational displays, if installed, to monitor position in relation to the desired flightpath during holding.

B. TASK: HOLDING PROCEDURES

REFERENCES: 14 CFR part 91; FAA-H-8083-9, FAA-H-8083-15; FAA-S-ACS-8, FAA-S-ACS-14; AIM.

Objective. To determine that the applicant:

1. Exhibits instructional knowledge of holding procedures by describing—

   a. setting of aircraft navigation equipment.
   b. requirement for establishing the appropriate holding airspeed for the aircraft and altitude.
   c. recognition of arrival at the holding fix and the prompt initiation of entry into the holding pattern.
   d. timing procedure.
   e. correction for wind drift.
   f. use of DME in a holding pattern.
   g. compliance with ATC reporting requirements.

2. Exhibits instructional knowledge of common errors related to holding procedures by describing—

   a. incorrect setting of aircraft navigation equipment.
   b. inappropriate altitude, airspeed, and bank control.
   c. improper timing.
   d. improper wind drift correction.
   e. failure to recognize holding fix passage.
   f. failure to comply with ATC instructions.

3. Demonstrates and simultaneously explains holding procedures from an instructional standpoint.

4. Analyzes and corrects simulated common errors related to holding procedures.

5. Exhibits instructional knowledge on the use of the MFD and other graphical navigational displays, if installed, to monitor position in relation to the desired flightpath during holding.

VIII. AREA OF OPERATION: INSTRUMENT APPROACH PROCEDURES

NOTE: The evaluator shall select TASKS A and B, to be combined with TASK C, D, or E. At least one nonprecision approach procedure shall be accomplished without the use of the gyroscopic heading and attitude indicators under simulated instrument conditions. Circling approaches are not applicable to helicopters.

A. TASK: NONPRECISION INSTRUMENT APPROACH (NPA)

REFERENCES: 14 CFR part 91; FAA-H-8083-9, FAA-H-8083-15; FAA-S-ACS-8, FAA-S-ACS-14; IAP; AIM.

The evaluator has discretion to have the applicant perform a landing or a missed approach at the completion of each approach.

Objective. To determine that the applicant:

1. Exhibits instructional knowledge of the elements of a nonprecision instrument approach by describing—

    a. selection of the appropriate instrument approach procedure chart.
    b. pertinent information on the selected instrument approach chart.
    c. radio communications with ATC and compliance with ATC clearances, instructions, and procedures.
    d. appropriate aircraft configuration, airspeed, and checklist items.
    e. selection, tuning, identification, and determination of operational status of ground and aircraft navigation equipment.
    f. adjustments applied to the published MDA and visibility criteria for the aircraft approach category.
    g. maintenance of altitude, airspeed, and track, where applicable.
    h. establishment and maintenance of an appropriate rate of descent during the final approach segment.
    i. factors that should be considered in determining whether:

        (1) the approach should be continued straight-in to a landing;
        (2) a circling approach to a landing should be made; or
        (3) a missed approach should be performed.

2. Exhibits instructional knowledge of common errors related to a nonprecision instrument approach by describing—

   a. failure to have essential knowledge of the information on the instrument approach chart.
   b. incorrect communications procedures or noncompliance with ATC clearances or instructions.
   c. failure to accomplish checklist items.
   d. faulty basic instrument flying technique.
   e. inappropriate descent below the MDA.

3. Demonstrates and simultaneously explains a nonprecision instrument approach from an instructional standpoint.
4. Analyzes and corrects simulated common errors related to a nonprecision instrument approach.
5. Exhibits instructional knowledge on the uses of the MFD and other graphical navigational displays, if installed, to monitor position, track, wind drift, and other parameters to maintain desired flightpath.

B. TASK: PRECISION INSTRUMENT APPROACH (PA)

REFERENCES: 14 CFR part 91; FAA-H-8083-9, FAA-H-8083-15; FAA-S-ACS-8, FAA-S-ACS-14; IAP; AIM.

Objective. To determine that the applicant:

1. Exhibits instructional knowledge of a precision instrument approach by describing—

   a. selection of the appropriate instrument approach chart.
   b. pertinent information on the selected instrument approach chart.
   c. selection, tuning, identification, and determination of operational status of ground and aircraft navigation equipment.
   d. radio communications with ATC and compliance with ATC clearances, instructions, and procedures.
   e. appropriate aircraft configuration, airspeed, and checklist items.
   f. adjustments applied to the published DH/DA and visibility criteria for the aircraft approach category.
   g. maintenance of altitude, airspeed, and track, where applicable.
   h. establishment and maintenance of an appropriate rate of descent during the final approach segment.
   i. factors that should be considered in determining whether:

(1) the approach should be continued straight-in to a landing;

(2) a circling approach to a landing should be made; or

(3) a missed approach should be performed.

2. Exhibits instructional knowledge of common errors related to a precision instrument approach by describing—

a. failure to have essential knowledge of the information on the instrument approach procedure chart.

b. incorrect communications procedures or noncompliance with ATC clearances.

c. failure to accomplish checklist items.

d. faulty basic instrument flying technique.

e. inappropriate application of DH/DA.

3. Demonstrates and simultaneously explains a precision instrument approach from an instructional standpoint.

4. Analyzes and corrects simulated common errors related to a precision instrument approach.

5. Exhibits instructional knowledge on the uses of the MFD and other parameters to maintain desired flightpath.

C. TASK: MISSED APPROACH

REFERENCES: 14 CFR part 91; FAA-H-8083-9, FAA-H-8083-15; FAA-S-ACS-8, FAA-S-ACS-14; IAP; AIM.

Objective. To determine that the applicant:

1. Exhibits instructional knowledge of a missed approach procedure by describing—

a. pertinent information on the selected instrument approach chart.

b. conditions requiring a missed approach.

c. initiation of the missed approach, including the prompt application of power, establishment of a climb attitude, and reduction of drag.

d. required report to ATC.

e. compliance with the published or alternate missed approach procedure.

f. notification of ATC if the aircraft is unable to comply with a clearance, instruction, restriction, or climb gradient.

g. performance of recommended checklist items appropriate to the go-around procedure.

h. importance of positive aircraft control.

2. Exhibits instructional knowledge of common errors related to a missed approach by describing—

    a. failure to have essential knowledge of the information on the instrument approach chart.
    b. failure to recognize conditions requiring a missed approach.
    c. failure to promptly initiate a missed approach.
    d. failure to make the required report to ATC.
    e. failure to comply with the missed approach procedure.
    f. faulty basic instrument flying technique.
    g. descent below the MDA prior to initiating a missed approach.

3. Demonstrates and simultaneously explains a missed approach from an instructional standpoint.
4. Analyzes and corrects simulated common errors related to a missed approach.
5. Exhibits instructional knowledge on the uses of the MFD and other graphical navigational displays, if installed, to monitor position and track to help navigate the missed approach.

D. TASK: CIRCLING APPROACH (AIRPLANE)

REFERENCES: 14 CFR part 91; FAA-H-8083-9, FAA-H-8083-15; FAA-S-ACS-8; IAP; AIM.

Objective. To determine that the applicant:

1. Exhibits instructional knowledge of the elements of a circling approach by describing—

    a. selection of the appropriate circling approach maneuver considering the maneuvering capabilities of the aircraft.
    b. circling approach minimums on the selected instrument approach chart.
    c. compliance with advisories, clearance instructions, and/ or restrictions.
    d. importance of flying a circling approach pattern that does not exceed the published visibility criteria.
    e. maintenance of an altitude no lower than the circling MDA until in a position from which a descent to a normal landing can be made.

2. Exhibits instructional knowledge of common errors related to a circling approach by describing—

    a. failure to have essential knowledge of the circling approach information on the instrument approach chart.

b. failure to adhere to the published MDA and visibility criteria during the circling approach maneuver.

c. inappropriate pilot technique during transition from the circling maneuver to the landing approach.

3. Demonstrates and simultaneously explains a circling approach from an instructional standpoint.

4. Analyzes and corrects simulated common errors related to a circling approach.

E. TASK: LANDING FROM A STRAIGHT-IN APPROACH

REFERENCES: 14 CFR part 91; FAA-H-8083-9, FAA-H-8083-15; FAA-S-ACS-8, FAA-S-ACS-14; IAP; AIM.

Objective. To determine that the applicant:

1. Exhibits instructional knowledge of the elements related to landing from a straight-in approach by describing—

   a. effect of specific environmental, operational, and meteorological factors.

   b. transition to, and maintenance of, a visual flight condition.

   c. adherence to ATC advisories, such as NOTAMs, wind shear, wake turbulence, runway surface, and braking conditions.

   d. completion of appropriate checklist items.

   e. maintenance of positive aircraft control.

2. Exhibits instructional knowledge of common errors related to landing from a straight-in approach by describing—

   a. inappropriate division of attention during the transition from instrument to visual flight conditions.

   b. failure to complete required checklist items.

   c. failure to properly plan and perform the turn to final approach.

   d. improper technique for wind shear, wake turbulence, and crosswind.

   e. failure to maintain positive aircraft control throughout the complete landing maneuver.

3. Demonstrates and simultaneously explains a landing from a straight-in approach from an instructional standpoint.

4. Analyzes and corrects simulated common errors related to landing from a straight-in approach.

IX. AREA OF OPERATION: EMERGENCY OPERATIONS

NOTE: The evaluator shall select at least one TASK. The evaluator shall omit TASKS C and D unless the applicant furnishes a multiengine airplane for the practical test, then TASK C or D is mandatory.

A. TASK: LOSS OF COMMUNICATIONS

REFERENCES: 14 CFR part 91; FAA-H-8083-9, FAA-H-8083-15; FAA-S-ACS-8, FAA-S-ACS-14; IAP; AIM.

Objective. To determine that the applicant exhibits instructional knowledge of the elements related to loss of communications by describing:

1. Recognition of loss of communications.
2. When to continue with flight plan as filed or when to deviate.
3. How to determine the time to begin an approach at destination.

B. TASK: APPROACH WITH LOSS OF PRIMARY FLIGHT INSTRUMENT INDICATORS

REFERENCES: 14 CFR part 91; FAA-H-8083-9, FAA-H-8083-15; FAA-S-ACS-8, FAA-S-ACS-14; IAP; AIM.

Objective. To determine that the applicant:

1. Exhibits instructional knowledge of the elements related to loss of primary flight instrument indicators by describing—

    a. recognition of inaccurate or inoperative primary instrument indicators and advising ATC and the evaluator.
    b. notification of ATC or evaluator anytime that the aircraft is unable to comply with an ATC clearance or whether able to continue the flight.
    c. importance of utilizing navigation equipment in an emergency situation and demonstrating a nonprecision approach without the use of primary flight instruments.

2. Exhibits instructional knowledge of common errors related to loss of primary flight instrument indicators by describing—

    a. recognition of failed system components that relate to primary flight instrument indication(s).
    b. failure to notify ATC of situation.

c. failure to transition to emergency mode/standby instrumentation.

3. Demonstrates and simultaneously explains loss of primary flight instrument indicators by conducting a non-precision approach without the use of these indicators.

4. Analyzes and corrects common errors related to loss of primary flight instrument indicators.

C. TASK: ENGINE FAILURE DURING STRAIGHT-AND-LEVEL FLIGHT AND TURNS (MULTIENGINE)

REFERENCES: 14 CFR part 91; FAA-H-8083-9; FAA-S-ACS-6; FAA-S-ACS-8; Aircraft Flight Manual.

Objective. To determine that the applicant:

1. Exhibits instructional knowledge of the elements related to engine failure during straight-and- level flight and turns, solely by reference to instruments, by describing—

   a. appropriate methods to be used for identifying and verifying the inoperative engine.

   b. technique for maintaining positive aircraft control by reference to instruments.

   c. importance of accurately assessing the aircraft's performance capability with regard to action that maintains altitude or minimum sink rate considering existing conditions.

2. Exhibits instructional knowledge of common errors related to engine failure during straight- and-level flight and turns, solely by reference to instruments, by describing—

   a. failure to recognize an inoperative engine.

   b. hazards of improperly identifying and verifying the inoperative engine.

   c. failure to properly adjust engine controls and reduce drag.

   d. failure to establish and maintain the best engine inoperative airspeed.

   e. failure to follow the prescribed checklist.

   f. failure to establish and maintain the recommended flight attitude for best performance.

   g. failure to maintain positive aircraft control while maneuvering.

   h. hazards of exceeding the aircraft's operating limitations.

   i. faulty basic instrument flying technique.

3. Demonstrates and simultaneously explains straight-and-level flight and turns after engine failure, solely by reference to instruments, from an instructional standpoint.
4. Analyzes and corrects simulated common errors related to straight-and-level flight and turns after engine failure, solely by reference to instruments.

D. TASK: INSTRUMENT APPROACH—ONE ENGINE INOPERATIVE (MULTIENGINE)

REFERENCES: 14 CFR part 91; FAA-H-8083-9; FAA-S-ACS-8, FAA-S-ACS-14, Aircraft Flight Manual.

Objective. To determine that the applicant:

1. Exhibits instructional knowledge of the elements related to an instrument approach with one engine inoperative by describing—

   a. maintenance of altitude, airspeed and track appropriate to the phase of flight or approach segment.
   b. procedure if unable to comply with an ATC clearance or instruction.
   c. application of necessary adjustments to the published MDA and visibility criteria for the aircraft approach category.
   d. establishment and maintenance of an appropriate rate of descent during the final approach segment.
   e. factors that should be considered in determining whether:

      (1) the approach should be continued straight-in to a landing; or
      (2) a circling approach to a landing should be performed.

2. Exhibits instructional knowledge of common errors related to an instrument approach with one engine inoperative by describing—

   a. failure to have essential knowledge of the information that appears on the selected instrument approach chart.
   b. failure to use proper communications procedures.
   c. noncompliance with ATC clearances.
   d. incorrect use of navigation equipment.
   e. failure to identify and verify the inoperative engine and to follow the emergency checklist.

f.   inappropriate procedure in the adjustment of engine controls and the reduction of drag.

g.   inappropriate procedure in the establishment and maintenance of the best engine inoperative airspeed.

h.   failure to establish and maintain the proper flight attitude for best performance.

i.   failure to maintain positive aircraft control.

j.   faulty basic instrument flying technique.

k.   inappropriate descent below the MDA or DH.

l.   faulty technique during roundout and touchdown.

3. Demonstrates and simultaneously explains an instrument approach with one engine inoperative from an instructional standpoint.

4. Analyzes and corrects simulated common errors related to an instrument approach with one engine inoperative.

X. AREA OF OPERATION: POSTFLIGHT PROCEDURES

A. TASK: CHECKING INSTRUMENTS AND EQUIPMENT

REFERENCES: FAA-S-ACS-8, FAA-S-ACS-14; Aircraft Flight Manual.

Objective. To determine that the applicant exhibits instructional knowledge of the elements related to checking instruments and equipment by describing:

1. Importance of noting instruments and navigation equipment for improper operation.
2. Reasons for making a written record of improper operation or failure and/or calibration of instruments prior to next IFR flight.

APPENDIX 1—FSTD Credit

TASK VS. FSTD CREDIT

Evaluators conducting the instrument rating practical tests with FSTDs should consult appropriate documentation to ensure that the device has been approved for training, testing, or checking, and assigned the appropriate qualification level in accordance with the requirements of 14 CFR part 60.

The FAA must approve the device for training, testing, and checking the specific flight TASKS listed in this appendix.

The device must continue to support the level of student or applicant performance required by this practical test standard.

If an FSTD is used for the practical test, the instrument approach procedures conducted in that FSTD are limited to one precision and one nonprecision approach procedure.

USE OF CHART

X Creditable
A Creditable if appropriate systems are installed and operating

NOTE: Users of the following chart are cautioned that the use of the chart alone is incomplete. The description and objective of each TASK as listed in the body of the practical test standard, including all NOTES, must also be incorporated for accurate FSTD use.

"Postflight Procedures" means closing flight plans, checking for discrepancies and malfunctions, and noting them on a log or maintenance form.

FLIGHT TASK - FSTD LEVEL

Areas of Operation	1	2	3	4	5	6	7	A	B	C	D
Preflight Procedures											
C. Instrument Flight Deck Check *				A	A	X	X	X	X	X	X
Air Traffic Control Clearances and Procedures											
A. ATC Clearances				A	A	X	X	X	X	X	X
B. Departure, En Route and Arrival Clearances *						X	X	X	X	X	X
Flight by Reference to Instruments											
A. Basic Instrument Flight Maneuvers						X	X	X	X	X	X
B. Recovery from Unusual Flight Attitudes							X	X	X	X	X
Navigation Aids											
A. Navigational Systems and DME Arcs					A	X	X	X	X	X	X
B. Holding Procedures						X	X	X	X	X	X
Instrument Approach Procedures											
A. Nonprecision Instrument Approach						X	X	X	X	X	X
B. PA						X	X	X	X	X	X
C. Missed Approach						X	X	X	X	X	X
D. Circling Approach								X	X	X	X
E. Landing from a Straight-in or Circling Approach									X	X	X
Emergency Operations											
A. Loss of Communications						X	X	X	X	X	X
B. One Engine Inoperative during Straight-and-Level Flight and Turns (Multiengine Airplane)						X	X	X	X	X	X
C. One Engine Inoperative—Instrument Approach (Multiengine Airplane)								X	X	X	X
D. Loss of Gyro Attitude and/or Heading Indicators						X	X	X	X	X	X
Postflight Procedures											
A. Checking Instruments and Equipment					A	X	X	X	X	X	X

* Aircraft required for those items that cannot be checked using a flight training device or flight simulator.